A Kindergarten Teacher
Looks at the Word
GOD

I0807602

A Kindergarten Teacher Looks at the Word GOD

Reflections
on Goodness, Oneness, and Diversity

By Betty Peck

Illustrated by Virginia Fordice

Rudolf Steiner College Press

Permission to use the photograph of the Helix Nebula NGC 7293 was kindly granted by NASA, NOAO, ESA, the Hubble Helix Nebula Team, M. Meixner (STScI), and T. A. Rector (NRAO).

Cover art: Virginia Fordice
Cover design: Betty Peck, Claude Julien and John Wihl

ISBN 978-0-945803-93-5

Book orders may be made through
The Bookstore at Rudolf Steiner College
Tel: 916-961-8729, FAX: 916-961-3032
Catalog and online orders: www.steinercollege.edu
E-mail: orders@steinercollege.edu

Rudolf Steiner College Press
9200 Fair Oaks Boulevard
Fair Oaks, CA 95628, USA

Acknowledgments

There would never be enough room to thank all those who have helped to produce this book. Publisher Claude Julien and editor Judy Blatchford from the Rudolf Steiner Press have made it all happen in ways I could not have imagined when I first began.

My husband, Willys Peck, is my personal editor for everything I write. His sense of humor and love of language, words, and the elements of style have always delighted and inspired me. My daughter, Anna Rainville, works closely with me at all times. We enjoy creating forums for teachers and parents and share our passion for early childhood education. My son, Bill, a high school English teacher, is continuously called by the muses of poetry and drama. I have been further blessed when creating this book by two beautiful granddaughters, Sarah and Merina, whose hugs and "I-love-you's" make every day a joy.

I am grateful for the many parents of past Kindergarten students who have enriched my life. One in particular, Virginia Fordice, has generously continued to share her artistic talents with me. My admiration for her work is the reason I chose her to illustrate this book. I am also thankful to Evan Winslow Smith, the graphic artist, and to John Wihl, project coordinator at the print shop in Sacramento, for their skills in manifesting the vision for this book.

How fortunate I am at the age of 86 to be supported and encouraged by a circle of friends in all the things of consequence. Artist and writer, Jade Bradbury, has for many years curated the essential personal and artistic aspects of my life, including helping to bring this book to fruition. Another artist friend, Pat Fox, has graced our home and garden over many years, inspiring me with her calligraphy and unique imagery. Kate Hendon's lovely soprano voice, spiritual teachings, and devoted attention to my health needs have been a welcome constant as this book unfolded. My dear friend, author and storyteller Nancy Mellon provided invaluable editorial assistance, as did Kate Hendon and Mert Parsons.

I would also like to thank the other people who help maintain the beauty of the historic home where I live: Kathleen Coakley, for general office management and for keeping the faith in our Saratoga community through dedicated political activism; John Towler, along with Nancy Lee, Kathryn Mathewson and the Helbush family, Rebecca and Hank—gardeners for all seasons in the Peck Heritage Garden. Carpenter, David Garcia, long ago one of my Kindergarten students, has continued to create well-crafted solutions for the inside and outside of our house during the creation of this book.

Bill Kalogeros and Don Armstrong have been my computer geniuses, always there to answer my questions and offset my technological errors. April Halberstadt helped me to explore the publishers of small books. I would be remiss not to mention the Thursday Salon regulars whose enthusiasm for my book idea inspired the Reflections and Meditations sections of the book. May the many others of you who have contributed to this book know who you are. I am deeply grateful to each and every one of you.

Blessings,
Betty Peck

Publisher's Preface

Betty Peck began with a strong wish and intention to help the children of the world come to know what is good and true and beautiful through the wonders of nature and the human treasures to be found in the cultures of all peoples. After over fifty years of teaching young children, the essence of that experience crystallized for her as a new way of understanding the word GOD.

In turn, Virginia Fordice transformed this concept into a finely painted triptych that incorporates archetypes from mythology with lovely elements from the four kingdoms of nature. A representation of this artistic piece is included inside the back cover of the book.

Betty shared this gift from the children with friends who found meditative inspiration in it; they took it into their varied life experiences and gave enthusiastic responses that shed light from diverse directions. Out of her deep concern for the world today, Betty invites each reader to join in the dialogue and to help spread the word.

Foreword

The incomparable Betty Peck is one of the most delightful and wonderfully original Kindergarten teachers I have ever met. Like the wise grandmother elder in this little book of GOD, pouring out her cornucopia of abundance and beauty, Betty has graced the world of childhood with her magic stardust of enthusiasm for life, adventure, reverence, and joy. Given to drama, wonder, and grand entrances, flowing capes and secret paths in the woods, Betty is the fairy godmother we all wished for.

Countless times, Betty has led happy troops of lucky children through fields and flowers on journeys of discovery of nature's bounty, of everything from bird nests to butterflies. She has lifted the youngsters with the wonder of the sounds and shapes of letters and brought them the beauty of poetry and the well-spoken word. Underlying all her teaching is her commitment to profound artistic educational philosophies, to Froebel and Rudolf Steiner's Waldorf education, to sterling ideals strongly held and expressed with a merry heart.

My favorite stories of Betty include her adamant insistence that the Nativity story belongs to everyone because, after all, whenever a child of God is born anywhere, surely angels sing, shepherds bow, and kings are ready to offer their gifts!

One time she confronted a man who demeaned the fantasy and imagination of childhood as unscientific and unnecessary. She countered with a question that surprised him. "Have you ever enjoyed a sunset or sunrise?" "Of course," the puzzled man answered. Then armed with the scientific fact that the sun never sets or rises, she airily rejoined, "Pure fantasy, my dear, pure fantasy!"

With all her teaching experience, Betty has taken the mentoring and inspiring of young teachers as a mission. For years she has offered Kindergarten Forums in her home, an enchanted place brimful of antiques and wondrous artifacts, and even a Great Hall with a stage for Shakespeare productions.

It is such a lovely gift Betty gives us with this little book of GOD, summing up a long, colorful, and caring career with a simple and elegant legacy of truth, goodness, and wisdom. May it be appreciated by many.

Nancy Jewel Poer
Waldorf Early Childhood Educator

How this book came to be

In the Kindergarten, I had the opportunity to polish and refine my beliefs and to practice my commitment to Goodness, Oneness, and Diversity. Yet it wasn't until after I retired from classroom teaching that I discovered what lives in the word GOD.

Never did I think of putting this philosophy of mine into the three letters that spell GOD in English until I began to feel that we all have a responsibility to find the solution to our worldwide problems. Why has war so often been waged? Why do we hear about it daily from the TV commentators and newspaper reporters? Does it have anything to do with their religious beliefs?

I realized that we could seek the answer in the way that I have discovered as a Kindergarten teacher: Young children have the answer if we but listen. Who then, or what, is GOD? Who is the God of our ancestors? Are we all referring to the same Source of Life? When I looked at the word God, this three-letter English name became more than alive. The thunder of its meaning struck me:

G is for Goodness
O is for Oneness of all life
D is for Diversity

I saw how this simple word offers strong, supporting roots for our lives today.

My next step was to find the right person to illustrate these three letters to show the wisdom they hold. My friend Virginia Fordice, whose five children had been in my Kindergarten and whose art work I admired, seemed to me to be the perfect artist for the job. When I asked her, she was shocked. "You have asked the wrong person to illustrate a book on God," she said. "I do not believe in God. I'm an atheist." "Yes," I replied, "you are just the one I want. You are more filled with life than any artist I know, and I love what you bring into your pictures." When I explained what I felt the English word God was holding for us all to discover, she said Yes. Being an atheist is somewhat closer to being a believer than one can imagine. Atheists care enough to question. The essence of God matters to them. And so, in her amazing studios in the Santa Cruz Mountains, she has beautifully painted with her watercolors the spiritual depth of each letter. I hope you will find the triptych she created as meaningful and inspiring as I have.

When I told others about the book, their comments were so wonderful that I asked them to write them down so they could be shared. They are included in the reflections section of this book. The final section of the book is a collection of quotations to spark further insight.

From the world of nature and the world of young children

At the age of 85, I feel the *Oneness* of all life, I know it to be true. I experience the oneness of all life when I look into the eyes of a child and feel again the wonder and awe that matches my own. Adults often come up to me and tell me how beautiful I am. And I say to them, "My dear, I feel I hold a mirror for you to see yourself. Look how beautiful you are. It is our spirits that feel oneness."

The Saratoga Creek runs through our property. On one side are the untamed woods, and on the other is my garden. Being in my garden and in nature fills my heart with gratitude, and I feel at one with the earth. In fact, I am often asked by different organizations to dress up as Mother Earth for their events and celebrations. I wish everyone could have this opportunity.

In the garden, I experience the intricacies of *Diversity*. The roots, the stems, the buds, the composition of the soil, the flowers and trees—everything belongs—everything contributes to the whole. In my Kindergarten class, I never hesitated to express my delight at the abundance of diversity. The ways in which we are the same and different gave me permission to embrace each nationality as my own. I love the different languages. I love the varied styles of dress. I love the many cultures and have tried to learn as much as I could from each one. I love diversity on all levels. I always like to say Yes before saying No.

Although I acknowledge the difficulty and trials of this life, I have chosen to say Yes to the *Good.* As a gardener, I know the power of the seed. When I look at a child, I can see the beauty that is not limited to that moment, for I believe in the inherent goodness that is the birthright of this child. As a teacher, I feel it is my duty to cultivate every possible seed of goodness and beauty. I know that my passion and belief inspires and protects each child. Each aspect of my Kindergarten program is based on belief in the intrinsic truth and goodness.

Photo by George Sakkestad

Betty and Willys Peck at home

Experiences with children in Kindergarten

I believe that you, too, would have come to the interpretation of GOD as Goodness, Oneness, and Diversity if you were teaching Kindergarten. Children recognize in their bones that we are all one. They delight in diversity as they play and celebrate. Bathed in myths and fairy tales, they feel the goodness that brings forth on all levels our gratitude for the gifts that are freely given to us.

Young children do not need the word "God." They are too busy drinking in the wonder of life and feeling the pulsation of the universe within and around them to reduce it all to one word. The child lives in imagination, movement, song, and drama that then explode into drawings. I always taught children to know their whole world before knowing printed black and white words.

In other words, young children develop gradually as the earliest human beings did. It is the teacher's job to see that the child is not cheated out of any of these developmental stages. It is the teacher's job to educate the parents and administrators about child development, while at the same time continuing to learn from the children. In his or her first seven years, the child is open to receive the foundation of every later phase of life.

Everything we do in Kindergarten reveals our oneness with all life. One way we become conscious of this is through counting. We start by using our fingers—as early human beings did. We start with the pointer finger as "one." Each successive finger is given its number, and the thumb crossing over the others is the "five." Next, in using these "finger numbers," we notice a shortcut as the Romans did—using the V formed between the thumb and forefinger as five. The children learn about the other numbers represented in their bodies. The teacher shows that, when we stand tall with our hands at our sides, we are pictures of the "one."

We also experience oneness in our bodies through our written language. The M of "mountains" is written on our lips. We can stand as a "king" in the form of the K with a crown on our head, our right arm raised and our right leg extended.

Children actually delight not only in the oneness of all life but also in the diversity that is found in the garden and classroom. I grew up in a family that did not feel at ease with cultural differences. Prejudice was painfully evident. However, through my own curiosity and the wisdom of trusted mentors, I discovered a new delight and ease in meeting people from different cultures and beliefs. In the Kindergarten we celebrated each child's culture. The following stories will give some idea of the wide range of new experiences that we encountered:

> One year, soon after school had started, one child went home and told her mother she did not want to come to Mrs. Peck's Kindergarten because she had only five-pointed stars there, and her synagogue had six-pointed stars. I said, "Please let her come early, and I will show her why I have five-pointed stars in my Kindergarten." When she arrived the next morning, a large piece of gold paper was on the floor. I said to her, "I am so sorry that you didn't know why I have five-pointed stars; lie down on the gold paper and I will show you." I then drew a star point around her head, one around each of her outstretched arms, and another around each of her outstretched legs. When she stood up, she saw the five-pointed star. I said, "You see, my dear, you are the reason I have five-pointed stars in

my Kindergarten." As the other children began to come in, they all wanted their own five-pointed stars. One little girl said, "I think I was born a five-pointed star."

I called them over to the Mother's Lap, my big overstuffed chair, and said, "I want to tell you the story of a king who wanted his own star. His name was King David. One day King David looked down from his castle window and saw all his beautiful five-pointed stars sweeping and cleaning his kingdom, and he said, 'I think I should have my own star. Let me see: What are the most important things in my kingdom? They are the sun, the moon, and the stars. And what are the most important things in my family?—my father, my mother and me. We are a family.' When he counted these important things in his family and in his kingdom, there was a six-pointed star." Then I told the children, "King David wants me to give you a gift that you are to plant six inches deep anywhere in the garden."

The children hurried around making six-inch rulers. They soon forgot the story and where they had planted their gift, until one day when someone saw a straight green blade coming from the spot where King David's gift had been planted. "Oh, it must be his sword," someone said. Then the daffodil bloomed, and they counted six petals. One child said, "Look, his crown is in the middle."

Another time, I wanted to celebrate the beautiful traditions of one of my Japanese students. When I told her mother that I planned to take the class to the beautiful Hakone Garden to celebrate her Japanese culture, she was shocked and said that she was not Japanese; she was an American. Her family did not speak Japanese, eat Japanese food, or keep the old traditions. I said, "You are Japanese, and we are going to celebrate your beautiful heritage." We made Japanese kimonos, we learned Japanese dances, and we did Japanese brush painting with an old Japanese grandmother. Tonso, the Japanese gardener, showed us how to count in Japanese. The mother became more Japanese than Japanese.

A third story relates to our land, which once belonged to the Ohlone tribe. We have found mortars in our creek where acorns were ground. Big Buffalo, a Native American, made us a big drum. He called *Spring* for us on his drum, and then he beat our Iroquois name *Saratoga*, which means Floating Scum upon the Water. In Saratoga, California, we live near a mineral spring like the one in Saratoga, New York. We also became Native Americans in our costumes and beat the rhythms of our own names on the drum. We found we could dance to these rhythms. Later we drew the patterns made by the rhythms and made necklaces with our name patterns.

We celebrated the spring New Year with another student from Iran. That beautiful ceremony is described in my Kindergarten book. We loved being a part of each other's family traditions and learning all the different ways of saying "I love you!" I always made it clear whenever I drew something that we are all artists. Because we are all artists, we will do our drawings in our own way. The children delighted in being different.

Most of all, we felt the awe and wonder of goodness—all the good things we shared together. Children can feel the good. They know they are part of the oneness of all life. They delight in diversity.

The Kindergarten Teacher's Creed

I bring the gift of myself
To this celebration of life
We call the Kindergarten.

I come each day
To be refined, smoothed, tempered,
For I hold in my hands,
With wonder and gratitude,
The future!

Seeds of the future are in the oneness
Of all nature and all people
In tune with the divine to be found in our hearts
That I give, through the joy and beauty of love.

Betty Peck

pf

Betty Peck on May Day

My story

My father and mother met at a Baptist Church in San Francisco when my father had his offices on Market Street. He owned Remolite Paint Company and my mother was a pianist and lab technician. I was born in 1921 and lived on Edgewood Avenue, one of the most beautiful streets in San Francisco. When I was a small child I became very ill, and the doctors were at a loss to know how to save me. My father was away on business. My mother heard on the radio that anyone who needed help could request prayers, and she phoned in. The next day two ladies came to ask about the child. My mother said, "Look, she is well!" The ladies explained that they had prayed for her sick child—the doctors were amazed—and invited her to attend Angeles Temple. My grateful mother took her children to see the great stories of the Old Testament dramatized on stage there by Aimee Semple McPherson. I remember re-delivering her colorful sermons when we got home each Sunday. As years went by, I felt that I knew personally each character in the Old Testament.

My Kindergarten teacher was chosen by the gods. My memories are still a delight to tell. That summer, the school district canvassed the neighborhood looking for five-year-old students for their Kindergarten. I would not be five until December, but they decided to accept me anyway. When my baby sister was born, the entire class was invited to see her. I remember my father standing with outstretched arms stopping the cars on Long Beach Boulevard so that the Kindergarten children could cross over to my house. They gathered around her crib to admire this beautiful baby and gave her the rattle they had brought as a gift for her. How proud I was at this moment! It was *my* baby sister, *my* mother, *my* father, *my* house, *my* world, *my* Kindergarten, and *my* teacher. The oneness of the world was mine.

I will always capitalize the word Kindergarten. This is how Froebel first wrote the word when he gave it to the world in 1865. When the concept of Kindergarten was brought over to America and added to grades 1 through 12, we dropped the capitalization to blend in with the naming of the other grades. It is time to revive the dignity of this important concept.

I moved with my family to Los Angeles when I was in the first grade. I remember running all the way home carrying my reading book. I had learned to read! When I reached home, I breathlessly rushed through the door to read the book to my mother. We sat in the nearest chair to the front door, and I read every word with pride and pleasure to my mother. When I was finished, my mother, who did not believe I could read, said, "Now, read it backwards!" And with more pleasure than before, I read every sentence backwards—for at that moment I realized that it was possible for me to know things my mother could not know. This feeling of separation and feeling the power of my own self has never left me. Reading is such an important step in the development of the human being, and I encourage parents to celebrate this moment.

At the school there was a gardening teacher with her own greenhouse. I remember kneeling down beside her as she taught me to transplant a pansy. She was wearing a black smock that caught the rays of the sun. My mother was much too busy to oversee our garden, so she let me be in charge. It was there that I observed trapdoor spiders and the wild grasses in the nearby vacant lots.

My mother often took us to the beach, to the mountains to gather poppies, or to a nearby park. We were always on an adventure—in the woods, at the sea fishing, being part of the beauty of the earth. When we moved to my father's ranch, we slept on hay wagons. Never before had I seen the black night with millions of stars flying across the sky. We are wrapped in the Milky Way.

At the Baptist Church, I found myself standing alone within the words of John 10:10, "I am come that you might have life and have it more abundantly." I became a John 10:10 Christian. Later, when I began teaching third grade at University Avenue School in Los Gatos, I found a Presbyterian minister who preached this message and chose him to perform our marriage ceremony, when Willys Peck and I wed in 1952.

For a time I was a supervisor for San Mateo County schools working with Kindergarten, first-, second-, and third-grade teachers. When my two children were born, I opened my own Kindergarten demonstration school under the auspices of the American Association of University Women. When our children were ready for nursery school, I opened a program for the education of parents and their young children on a farm with barns, animals, fields of fruit trees, and gardens. All the parents felt grateful for the gift of the beauty of nature for their children. This school has recently celebrated its 50th anniversary.

When my husband decided to go to law school, I was hired to teach Kindergarten in the public school here in Saratoga. I have never stopped reading and collecting information or sitting at the feet of those I feel have vital information that enriches one's soul. After several years, I was given the opportunity to develop my own Kindergarten program, which I have written about in my book, *Kindergarten Education: Freeing Children's Creative Potential* (Stroud, UK: Hawthorn Press, 2003).

A daughter's perspective

My mother defines the world with a "Yes!" She loves to draw close to the mysteries of life and chooses to find the deep beauty and goodness in everyone and everything. People sense that she believes in the deep essence of who they are. She loves ideas and goes to bed each evening with a stack of diverse books to read. She loves reading about those people whose lives hold brilliant beauty, goodness and truth. With any philosopher, educator, theologian, gardener, doctor, teacher who opens up a glimpse of the ultimate mysteries—that's where she wants to be. She never reads novels, because she says that her life is already too thrilling. She reads actively, with a pencil in hand taking note of what resonates with her philosophy of life. She often reads aloud to me over the telephone. She loves to study the evolution of ideas, how children learn, the mysteries of the natural world, why architects build, how to expand her interest in nutrition, macrobiotics and feng shui. She integrates into our home my father's long family history with China. My mother's wardrobe and decor reflect her passion for diversity; she wears traditional ethnic garments and high fashion from local artists. Her attire is woven together with family jewelry and the handcrafted objects she places lovingly in all the rooms of our family home.

My mother continues to create her garden, changing paths, shaping intriguing nooks. She recently built an archway for Kuan Yin. She makes her garden a living expression of who she is. She walks every day in the garden with my father. I think it reassures her of the lawfulness of life and the rightness of cycles. She identifies with the possibilities of a living garden and keeps working to create connections that sustain and enliven. She feels so at one with her garden that once, when she forgot to bring her usual rose to greet me at the airport, she flung out her arms and said, "I am the rose!"

My mother taught for more than fifty years, and it naturally followed that she would continue drawing close to the mysteries of life. Her courage to believe grants her remarkable power to take risks in expressing herself for the ideals she holds most dear. I was not surprised when she told me she was making a book about GOD. It seemed a natural progression from the inspirational book she wrote about her years in the classroom, *Kindergarten Education: Freeing Children's Creative Potential.* Throughout her life my mother has moved gracefully within and beyond the religious spectrum. She is grateful for her roots and continues to blossom, exploring many paths wherever she finds them—in books, places of worship, and meetings with old and new friends. I have witnessed her joy in the making of this book. Friends and former students have searched their beliefs in response to her call, creating a new life of community and blessing.

—Anna Rainville

Reflections on the concept

Goodness
Oneness
Diversity

Nathan Koren
Architect, studying for a business degree at Oxford

I was raised without much regard for God. To be honest, I had an innate disinclination to acknowledge the existence of my own biological parents—much less some invisible super-parent in the sky. I have heard of children who are apparently born with a tremendous sense of piety and devotion; that wasn't me.

Yet I gradually became aware that this alleged "God" person held a mysterious sway over much of the world. Around age 8, I tried attending a variety of churches, grilling the Sunday school teachers until they acknowledged that they didn't really have any satisfactory answers, and that "God" was essentially a means of passing the buck on to the Department of Perpetual Ineffability. My churchgoing days ended a few years later with the conviction that God, as an entity, was no more substantial than the Tooth Fairy or Santa Claus.

Moreover, unlike Santa Claus and such—who I was happy to play along with, on the theory that it was all in good fun, and that it might get me some loot—this whole God business had something sinister about it, I thought. People were always ardently making silly claims in the name of God—and worse, committing unending atrocities. Sometimes it seemed to me that the love of God had brought more evil into the world than the love of money and vengeance combined.

And yet... I couldn't deny that the world was sacred, that existence was more than a material and mechanistic phenomenon. There was an unmistakable holiness that I could see in the faces of others, in growing things, in the desert air, in music—in everyone, everywhere, everything. The source of all this divinity was a great mystery to me, too tantalizing to dismiss. Nor could I deny that "God" and his innumerable incarnations and institutions were often a profoundly positive influence for many people, allowing them to live peaceful and fulfilled lives. How could this be? My spiritual quest continued.

I tried my hand at non-deistic religion—Buddhism mostly—finding that it provided interesting tools for getting closer to the source of all this divinity. Certainly there was something truly profound, that I could almost touch when in the depths of meditation, where form and void become one and the same—but coming back to the concrete world, I wasn't sure what good this did. I had no personal interest in achieving enlightenment; to the extent that enlightenment is an all-consuming endeavor, to lust for it seemed rather narcissistic to me. Nor did I have any desire to escape from the world, to fall off the wheel of rebirth. I love the world, and would rather focus my energies on doing some good in it, rather than spend all my energy trying to meditate ever more perfectly.

So I tried nature-based religions next. More outwardly-focused than Buddhism, perhaps they would give me what I sought. Polytheism was reasonably amusing: to treat all gods respectfully and no god seriously, I thought, was certainly much better than some of the alternatives. In any event, the rituals were pleasingly action-oriented, in terms of manifesting goodness during this incarnation. Philosophically, I found that Pantheism—the notion that everything is divine, that everything is in essence part of God—came closer to the literal truth of the matter. But what did that really tell me—that infinity is equal to infinity? What good does it do to know this?

Parallel with my spiritual questing, I strove to understand science and the material world as well as I could, thinking that perhaps it could give me some clues to the nature of the great mystery. And truly, I often felt glimmers of understanding—akin to what I experienced during meditation or ritual—when contemplating the evolution of biospheres, or the nuances of fractal mathematics. Whatever it was that I was seeking, it could be found in all of these things, if only I could see more clearly.

I wish that I could say that I had a big "Aha!" moment, where all the pieces of the puzzle fell thunderously into place. But I didn't. Rather, I gradually began to understand that I was no longer seeking, because I had found my answer.

This isn't easy to write about; until this moment, I've never even tried. My hesitation is partly based on the conviction that this is not the answer—just my answer—an utterly personal and idiosyncratic way of apprehending the universe, my own individual way of understanding that which others could understand as God. I strongly believe—for reasons that will shortly become obvious—that other people can and should find entirely different answers for themselves. Moreover, although part of my answer is empirically based (upon an odd assortment of biology, cosmology, and mathematics), another part is based in trans-rational and subjective realms—that is, the non-verbal knowing that I've gleaned through meditation, ritual, and various other transcendent experiences. The rational parts are complex yet describable, but the rest can only be crudely approximated in writing, since human language is only a very small and limited subset of the cosmos as a whole.

I suppose that a creation story would be one time-honored way to describe my philosophy. So here's how my own personal creation story would go. To anyone who has kept up-to-date with contemporary cosmology, the beginning may sound somewhat familiar:

> Roughly 15 billion years ago, the universe existed as pure, singular, undifferentiated energy. There was no space, no matter, no time—just energy. All was one, and one was all.
>
> This was boring. So, space and time came into existence, and energy expanded to fill it up. As energy expanded, however, it cooled

and hardened, and bits of it began clumping together. Now the universe was no longer singular. It came in bits, and some of those bits were unlike other of those bits. For the first time, otherness came into existence. Where before there had been only one object and one quality—pure, undifferentiated energy—now there were an infinity of objects with two very different qualities. Let's call them quarks and gluons.

The instant that they came into being, quarks and gluons felt a powerful, inexorable attraction to one another, and they raced into an embrace, which they have been locked into ever since. But unity can never reverse what division has wrought, and the joining of quarks and gluons did not recreate the primordial singular energy of the universe. It created something even better.

From the embrace of quarks and gluons was born a host of fundamental particles: muons, leptons, neutrinos, electrons, positrons, and so forth. Again, these particles felt a profound attraction towards one another, and again they rushed towards union—and again, this resulted in a still greater diversity of particles: protons, neutrons, and then light elements of the universe.

As always, the individual bits of the universe sought to come together, always longing to return to that original state of absolute oneness. When the first atoms in the universe came together, as vast collapsing clouds of hydrogen and helium, they ignited into huge, hot-burning stars. And as always, the result of this attempted oneness was the rise of still more diversity. The first generation of stars exploded into vast clouds of more complicated atoms, giving rise to the heavier elements throughout the universe.

You can probably see where this is headed: the heavier elements, seeking oneness, form still more stars, and now planets too. Carbon atoms attempted to achieve oneness with their surroundings, resulting in the still-greater complexity of organic chemistry. On and on it goes, to amino acids, to autocatalytic enzymes, to protocellular communities, to cells, to—everyone's favorite—intergametic reproduction, to you and me, to our children.

As overwhelming and complicated as all of this sounds, it's really a dance with only two steps: union followed by differentiation, unity begetting diversity, oneness giving rise to the many, on and on forever. This is the recipe for creating the cosmos, the underlying force that literally binds the universe together; the pull which brings both subatomic particles and lovers together is one and the same. This process, to me, is the very heartbeat of God.

Creation stories, of course, are not particularly useful as literal accounts of "how we got here." Rather, they are useful as metaphorical blueprints for every act of creation—creation being the province of every being. In understanding that oneness and diversity are the absolute core values, in studying the myriad nuances of this two-step dance, and in striving for goodness by attempting to continue this dance in my own life, I find that my personal philosophy constantly offers me very specific insight and direction in the course of my life. In doing so, it lends my daily existence a sense of harmony and congruity with the universe as a whole.

I've always suspected that this is probably one of the more byzantine ways of learning to feel at peace with the universe. So imagine my surprise when my old Kindergarten teacher called me up to tell me that that G.O.D. = Goodness, Oneness, Diversity. I cannot possibly imagine a more perfect and succinct encapsulation of my own personal philosophy. I arrived at this philosophy via half a dozen religions and even more scientific disciplines; she apparently just decoded an acronym. Not that I haven't very much enjoyed my philosophical journey, but evidently I took the scenic route.

And I really do think that she's captured it: Oneness and Diversity are indeed the core components of creation, each meaningless without the other. They are the most fundamental steps of the cosmic dance. And where does Goodness fit in? To me, Goodness is that which seeks to honor both Oneness and Diversity wherever they are found, and to bring about more of both, in every way possible. To do that is to not only honor God, but to create it!

Debra Agee
Mother, Waldorf school teacher

I heard Archbishop Desmond Tutu say, "Good always wins!"
He should know.

God never tires of stimulating the goodness in humanity. God is goodness itself. We are intimately connected to God when we find the Goodness in others, in the world, and in ourselves. Our inner knowing responds with deep joy the more we focus on and act out of Goodness.

GOD in us—all of us—GOODNESS in us.

So be it!

At the heart and core of gOd is—ONENESS.

ONENESS is the Alpha and Omega of all existence, cosmic and earthly.

ONENESS is the conveyance and the path.

ONENESS permeates, harmonizes, and synthesizes all polarities.

Inner and outer become a seamless whole. Center point and periphery turn inside out eternally, one within the other within the ONE. Birth and Death breathe, each the beginning of the other, intimately informing the Dance of Existence. Time becomes Space, and Spirit is all there
IS.

In ONENESS,
the House of Mirrors—that conglomeration of silver, slivered nuance, which expresses the infinite fragmentation of our unenlightened egos—is transformed into the pure, transparent, numinous prism of the
I AM.

Then, ONENESS individuates for the sole purpose of magnifying the Truth of GOD, which resonates in us and through us.

Thus does diversity arise—it need not be feared or shunned.

When every flower in the Garden blossoms to its fullest, the wholeness that GOD IS is celebrated. Diversity then reminds us all in infinite ways of the magnanimous manifest Creation. Every expression of the Creation can deliver us to GOD. GOD is generous, abundant, and patient. And, HE is waiting for us!

Thus, to the top of the highest mountain all paths stream. From the Crowning Peak all humanity is *seen, embraced, and loved.*

BY GOD, FOR GOD, WITH GOD, IN GOD, OF GOD

SO BE IT!

Just as GOD streams through all aspects of Creation, out of Oneness, from Goodness through Diversity, so does the impulse that is GOD stream and weave in and out of the energy that embraces and emanates from this little book. One might ask: to whom is this book directed? Initially, seeing that it is brought by a Kindergarten teacher, it might seem obvious that the answer is *children.*

The young child, however, does not need such a reminder. To wit, the four-year old who asks his parents for some "alone time" with the new infant sister who is lying in her crib. The parents are slightly alarmed and concerned. Will this encounter be one of rivalry and harm? Should they allow the brother to be with her alone, unsupervised? Not wanting to set suspicion in motion, and wanting to grant the moment to their son, they agree. The baby monitor will be on, after all, and the parents can be in the room in a heartbeat if things go awry. Imagine the parents bent over the monitor's speaker, listening intently. And brother says to his new baby sister, "Quick, tell me what it is like up in heaven, I have almost forgotten."

We adults can find our way to GOD only to the extent that we can become as little children. Let this "simple little book" be a gentle yet profound reminder that every single one of us, both the intellectual sophisticates among us and the more simple-hearted, are nothing less than children of GOD. The signs of the times are begging us to wake up to this reality. I have spent much of my life waiting for GOD—only to discover that GOD, always and forever there/HERE—has been waiting for me.

Thank you, Betty, for shepherding our attention HERE.

Joseph Houston
Optical scientist

As an astronomer and one who builds telescopes, I feel that God, the Great Creator, has always been there. If we accept that from energy there was light, and that from light there was our universe, then God's creation is our origin. If we also believe that we have a soul, then there must be a destination for this soul after all of the hydrogen and helium in our universe has been exhausted. As the science fiction author David Darling describes this destination in his book, *Deep Time*, it is a "pool of souls." [The text of this entire work is available at www.daviddarling.info/works/DeepTime.]

Although ideas about the birth of our universe and the origin of life in our universe require us to make a leap of faith, these ideas are based on scientific evidence and an understanding of how this evidence fits into a much bigger picture. This same leap of faith is a part of our desire to reach out beyond the planet Earth and look to the heavens. One has only to look at the night sky through a telescope and see the distant galaxies in order to experience the awesome beauty of our universe and feel the presence of the Great Creator. Isaiah said (40:26): Lift your eyes and look to the heavens. Who created all of these? He who brings out the starry host one by one and calls them each by name. He is worthy of our wonder, for his glory is higher than the heavens.

One of the beautiful sights seen through the lens of the Hubble Telescope and composited with images from Kitt Peak in Arizona is the awe-inspiring object called "Eye of God." An explanation copied from the HST web site describes this object as follows: The Helix Nebula is the closest example of a planetary nebula created at the end of the life of a Sun-like star. The outer gases of the star expelled into space appear from our vantage point as if we are looking down a helix. The remnant central stellar core, destined to become a white dwarf star, glows in light so energetic it causes the previously expelled gas to fluoresce. Will our Sun look like this one day? (See image on back cover of this book.)

Astronomy serves as a common bond between all individuals, regardless of race or religion, and provides us with a means of communicating with one another and with the Great Creator. In the language of astronomy, we can take the letter G to stand for Goodness and the ultimate Gift of life provided by the Great Creator to the dwellers of this Universe. The letter O stands for Oneness—the Universe—defined as the totality of all things that exist: creation, the cosmos, the whole world. The letter D stands for Diversity, which is another word for variety and reflects the differences among the creatures, great and small, who inhabit our universe…for we are not alone. We know that we come from the dust of the stars. We understand that the seeds of life were transported to the planet Earth by comets and asteroids. It takes only a small leap of faith to realize that from this single beginning we evolved and migrated to a variety of future homelands on our planet, taking with us a common ancestry as we multiplied into a diverse population. With this diversity in life forms and homelands we became many cultures. We developed myths and truths not only to survive, but also to sustain our belief in a Great Creator. This same leap of faith allows us now to accept the diversity of life and to become a part of the Universal Soul which is the basis of this life.

Katherine L. Hendon
Musician, writer, teacher

The various spiritual traditions of the world often remind us that the most valuable truths on the spiritual path are ones of great simplicity, condensed with wisdom which we may seek to unfold as part of our spiritual journey. Betty's three-word rendering of the notion of God is one example of such a truth. In contemplating this threefold symbolic representation, perhaps we might see in it a correspondence to the Divine Trinity of Aspects, common in all the spiritual traditions of the world yet known by many different names. On the most universal level—and the level to which this book speaks, I think—this Trinity of Aspects is known as Spirit/Soul/Matter or Life/Consciousness/Form. Some spiritual traditions even go so far as to suggest that this Trinity can be used to describe the nature of God. In this Divine Trinity of Aspects, Spirit refers to the breath of life, the energy which animates all creation. This Spirit is One in all of nature; it embodies oneness (O).

Matter/Form refers to the manifestation of Spirit in physical form. As we may readily observe in nature, this form is infinitely diverse: Spirit takes form in multiplicity or diversity (D).

The way that Spirit manifests through Form is through the medium of the Soul, just as a child or Son is born through the meeting of Spirit/Father and Matter/Mother. Every human being is a soul, a spark of spirit, manifesting through physical form. The biblical truism that we are all sons of God may thus be restated as: we are all Souls of God, expressing the Spirit of God through human form.

The nature of the soul is pure love. Love unites us with all other souls. Love serves to remind us that we are in essence One Soul, one with the souls of all lives—human, subhuman, and divine. In practical expression, love may also be described as the will-to-good, or goodwill towards all beings. Thus *God is good* (G) resonates with another deep truth which was and is the basic teaching of Christ, namely that *God is Love.*

Might we, then, dare to describe God as the synthesis of these three fundamental elements in manifestation in our solar system: Life, the One Soul, and Form? God's form is our universe as we know it. God's soul is the consciousness of the Logos Who brought our universe into being. God's spirit is that aspect of God which is ultimately transcendent, abstracted, and beyond the confines of our solar system. Our goal as self-realized human beings is to live the "One" within the "many," always remembering that our spirit aspect is one with the Spirit or Life aspect of God, and that while the One does manifest in infinite diversity, It remains eternally all-pervading, unchanged, and ultimately beyond any human naming.

Jade Bradbury
Artist, writer, museum curator

A Kindergarten Teacher Looks at the Word God, is Betty Peck's gift to a world much in need of its simple, perfect wisdom. In her own loving way she has re-visioned the word "God" as an acronym for the answer to what is universally right and true about the blessing of our shared lives on earth. As both my Native American and Celtic ancestors have maintained from earliest times, we are indeed all *One*. Pretty much of a piece here on Earth, it turns out that we are all children of the stars. Be we animal, mineral, or vegetable, we can trace our root ancestry to the stars, and know that congenital stardust tells the story of our carbon-based genesis. In broader terms, what this means is inescapable: that we are all related, interconnected by a cosmic web that exceeds even our most optimistic grasp of its intimations.

> …there is real power in joined voices. It is the power of human nature reweaving the sacred web of light, acknowledging the whole community. All we see is a reflection of consciousness, and to see requires pulling veils from the eyes, pulling away illusions that limit us in time and space, the illusions that say we are separate. We are not separate. We are all together. When we join our hearts in prayer, in singing, in sacred dancing, in planting things together, we are returning something to the Earth, planting seeds of good cause.
>
> *Dhyani Ywahoo*
> *Traditional Etowah Band of Eastern Tsalagi (Cherokee) Nation*

> The Universe is but one great city full of beloved ones, divine and human, by nature endeared to each other.
>
> *Epictetus*
> *Greek stoic philosopher, first century A.D.*

On another, more temporal but no less urgent level, I am a visual artist and a writer who especially treasures what we of like mind on Earth define as "the art of the book, the book as art." Betty's *God* book is not only beautifully conceived as succinct literature, but is about as wondrously illustrated by artist Virginia Fordice as her friend Betty—or any one of us—can imagine. This was a collaboration that could perhaps have only been made in heaven! I do wish that everyone could have been present in the Peck residence Great Hall one fine afternoon when Virginia relayed to us the back-story of how Betty persuaded her to "illuminate" the examination of a word whose letters spell G—O—D.

Beginning with seemingly antithetical philosophical positions, these two artists—writer and painter—created a visual definition that encompasses all and denies none. "The heart has its reasons...," and this is the point. How else shall we exist if not by becoming co-creators—artists—in the image of the Creator, the Great Spirit? We can do no less and expect no more.

Finally, and this is the sweet spot—the thing that makes each breath drawn, ever extending upward toward the sun, all of the flowing beneath the earth's crust, the passing of seasons, the surging and ebbing of galaxies and the incomprehensible birthing and dying of new stars above—the truth we recognize with complete humility and gratitude is everywhere for us to discover: We are loved, loving, and the expression of love incarnate. Whatever we do, for whatever reason, whatever we think or however we behave, this is our birthright and our legacy. What Betty's vision of God reminds us is that we are at home in the universe of relatedness; we have only to recognize and honor it. In that spirit we can be at peace and therefore actually make peace, the possibility of which is also written in our DNA, regardless of how we may believe ourselves to be "hard-wired." I am personally awed by what the subtext of Betty's book quietly suggests I consider about the nature of God, the universe, and ourselves:

> You may call God love, you may call God goodness. But the best name for God is compassion.
>
> *Meister Eckhart*
> *13th century German philosopher and mystic*

Bill Kalogeros
Senior network security analyst, veteran

Betty Peck's exploration of the word GOD is a much-needed reflection on what God is about. As the world gets smaller through our use of technology, the world's people and religions are running further apart and the world is becoming a very angry place. Who better than this elder of good wisdom, with the vision of the world through children's eyes, to take a look at GOD? Betty has taught, led, inspired, and loved generations of children—and has been an example to us adults of how to be better, more caring, loving, and respectful people.

As a Native American (Chiricahua Apache) and pipe carrier, I am honored to be asked to comment on this book. I am Apache by blood, but have been taught traditional Lakota spirituality and the Lakota ways. Those of us who have not been able learn all of our own ways look at the teachings of Lakota spirituality as a strong path for all of us displaced First Nations people in North America to follow. Our various traditions are blended and practiced at Pow-Wows across the U.S. From the Grand Entry to the dances and storytelling and healing ceremonies in the evenings, the traditions are still alive at the extended family level. What I will do here is tie our traditional teachings to Betty's words.

In the Lakota *tiyospayes* (extended families), children were regarded as sacred, of primary importance, and they received much of the *tiyospaye*'s attention. In fact, the word for child in the Lakota language is *wakan yeja* ('sacred being'). For the Lakota—and all First Nations peoples—the responsibility of raising a child was given to the entire community, and not just limited to a child's mother and father. As it is said in a Lakota proverb: The ones that matter the most are the children. The Lakota holy man Black Elk said:

> Grown men can learn from very little children—for the hearts of little children are pure. Therefore, the Great Spirit may show them many things that older people miss. A child is the greatest gift from Wakan Tanka (Great Spirit).

Good: Wakan Tanka, as Grandfather, is the Great Spirit—independent of manifestation, unqualified—and is compared to the Christian Godhead. Wakan Tanka, as Father, is the Great Spirit considered in relation to His manifestation as Creator, Preserver, or Destroyer, again comparable to the Christian God. In this same way, we are taught to live with two guide words (our two commandments): Honor and Respect. If we live our lives with honor and respect, everything falls into place. It allows us to look at all things with beauty and love.

Oneness: Betty's understanding of oneness is in keeping with our spiritual teachings as well. She says we are related to the oneness of others, and we have the same sacred saying: *Mitakuye Oyasin* ('we are all related'). When we do any task, we always try to do it in balance—if we take something, we also give back. A good example is when we cut down the willow branches used for our sacred (sweat) lodge for prayers, we offer tobacco, thanks, and prayers to the willows for making the sacrifice of themselves for us—again, we are all connected. In the days of the buffalo, this was always done before a hunt, and then afterward prayers and thanks were given back to the animals for their sacrifice. Black Elk taught us:

> You have noticed that everything an Indian does is in a circle, and that is because the power of the world always works in circles, and everything tries to be round. The sky is round and I have heard that the Earth is round like a ball and so are all the stars. The wind, in its greatest power, whirls. Birds make their nests in circles for theirs is the same religion as ours. Even the seasons form a great circle in their changing and always come back again to where they were. The life of a man is a circle from childhood to childhood and so it is in everything where power moves.

Chief Standing Bear also talked about the oneness:

> From Wakan Tanka, the Great Spirit, there came a great unifying life force that flowed in and through all things—the flowers of the plains, blowing winds, rocks, trees, birds, animals—and was the same force that had been breathed into the first man. Thus all things were kindred, and were brought together by the same Great Mystery.

Diversity: In the words of Black Elk:

> All birds, even those of the same species, are not alike, and it is the same with animals and with human beings. The reason Wakan Tanka does not make two birds, or animals or human beings exactly alike is because each is placed here by Wakan Tanka to be an independent individuality and to rely upon itself.

Kinship with all creatures of the earth, sky, and water was a real and active principle. In the animal and bird world there was a brotherly feeling that kept the Lakota safe among them. Some of the Lakota came so close to their feathered and furred friends that in true brotherhood they spoke a common tongue.

This observation about diversity by Betty is the most important concept of all. The world is at a crossroads right now. Instead of embracing our differences, the world's people are using their differences (political, religious and cultural) to drive deeper divides between people. Grandmother (the earth) continues to heat up from global warming, and we continue to lose more and more species (animal and plant) to extinction. We have to begin to embrace our differences and begin the healing process or we and, most importantly, our children will lose this precious legacy called earth—home.

I can't even imagine what a herd of 10,000 buffalo on the plains looked like to my ancestors. Just imagine that in only one more generation, if we don't begin the healing process, our grandchildren may wonder what it was like to see harbor seals, ducks, or even spring blossoms. We have to change our attitudes and perceptions about others and the earth. Betty's book is a good start.

Joan Phelan
Kindergarten teacher

Holly stood transfixed, as the jay bathed in the Kindergarten birdbath. Though she stood about ten feet away from the fluttering and splashing, Holly was totally at one with the blueness, the fluffed, wet feathers, as well as the greens, browns, yellows of the garden itself. I knew I was privy to something holy.

Young children are our reminder, our constant teachers about God. This is especially true when they are outdoors, especially in a garden. During my last six or eight years as a Kindergarten teacher, I was able to come to know this not only intellectually, but with every fiber of my being. Our Kindergarten garden butted right up against the asphalt of a typical public school playground. That play area was a monoculture of asphalt, sand, and steel. The play in that area consisted primarily of chasing and yelling—except when we added the natural element of water. Then, many of the children would stop their frenzied play to crouch down to mold the sand into rivers, peninsulas, and islands. Many would take journeys into the nearby garden to gather sticks, berries, leaves and pebbles to embellish their designs. Their voices became more quiet, their play, cooperative. Their natural goodness had the chance to flower.

In the garden itself children could find nooks and crannies to make fairy houses, and create fairy communities with tiny swimming pools, grocery stores, and schools. Other children found the bower under the cotoneaster perfect for reliving fairy tales we had been imagining in our classroom. The garden became the stage for reliving the ancient tales' lessons of generosity, taking care of one another, and listening to their deepest selves. In the garden, the children were immersed in diversity. They drank it in. They saw the different types of butterflies and saw which flowers each type of butterfly loved best. They discovered that there are different types of bees, big plants that provide cozy, shady places for other plants, and that some plants need to be off by themselves.

Mother Earth visited our classroom every winter solstice. She was a friend of mine, a true crone who knew the importance of children, the earth, and the holy. She appeared in costume and transformed sheep's wool into yarn on her spinning wheel, all the time singing and telling ancient stories. At the end of our time with her, Mother Earth gave each child his or her "Earth job." ...Edgar, would you please take care of the ladybugs? ...Taevia, your job is to take care of the north wind. ...Angelica, please watch over the sparkles on the water.

After Mother Earth left, we would gather together and talk about our important jobs. One year Jesse listened intently as his friends recited their jobs: to protect the flowers, take care of the bees, and welcome the morning sun. Jesse became very quiet, then looked at me and his Kindergarten friends and said, "It's all connected! All of these things are connected!"

Now that is certainly knowing God!

Daniel Bittleston
Educator, editor of *Imagination Troubadour*

In the work of Rudolf Steiner, we find many indications of how we can work together with the hierarchies of Intelligence to create a worthy future for our world. In fact, many great individualities, from Gandhi to Vonnegut, have shown ways. I heard Marshall Rosenberg a few days ago describing a world without rewards and punishments, a non-violent language of the heart, and the joy of compassionate giving. A truly gentle, caring, courageous man. I felt that God was alive in his every word.

Walking with a student of Emerson College in 1971, I remember she happened to mention God, and I exploded: "You say 'God' as though you were saying 'bus ticket'! Only when the concepts behind your words are deep, do they resonate."

In Shakespearean times, angels were called Intelligences. It was understood that the creation of Time required considerable intelligence. Space also. And Light. And how about Movement? I remember looking at a yellow and blue striped Fijian fish and saying to myself: Just who thought of that? Later, I spent quite a bit of time marveling at the creation of Consciousness. So, our Elizabethan ancestors were not yet taking all the wonders of nature and spirit for granted, as we generally do today. They pictured worlds of Intelligence within and around us, higher and higher Intelligences, filled with power and love, permeating and maintaining our planet.

The only thing that did not exist in the original majestic spiritual worlds was Freedom. Yet eternity and infinity were so overflowing with wisdom and generosity that mighty Intelligences gave their precious essences to create humankind, to give Love in Freedom a chance to evolve. And here we are.

And what is the name that we give the superabundant Intelligences that pour Wisdom, Life, and Love into every existing thing, from the beginning to the end of Time, and within each moment? Well, at one time it was considered dangerous to say GOD. (I hope in future you hear some kind of bell the size of Saturn sounding out when you read that word!)

Just a little research can show us that there are now no fewer than nine hierarchies of Intelligence in the world and human existence, and perhaps to our surprise, we can discover that in their amazing Diversity, they work together as One, with unfailing Goodness.

Jerome Parsons
Mechanical and control systems engineer

My training and experience are aligned with systems thinking in engineering—understanding problems and looking for solutions in a context larger than the issue itself. Understanding the larger context has always been vital to finding viable solutions in my experience. When I look at the many problems facing humankind and our planet today, I can think of no larger context than GOD—Good, Oneness, Diversity—manifested as a never-ending story.

G the Good: Everyone is born with a built-in knowing of what "doing good" means. It is held in the depths of our inner being. When we act out of that deeply held sense, those acts truly are *doing good.* But the Good is much more than that. It is an unconditional giving back, or maybe it's giving forward. Receiving the gifts of our universal story preceding us, adding our own true spirit and creativity, and giving forward to that which will follow after us. That pervasive true gifting from not just humans, but from Earth and from our universe, is how I think about the Good.

O the Oneness: Oneness is the interconnectedness, the interdependency of everything. Our own well-being is completely dependent on the well-being of so much around us—and within us. Oneness is very dynamic—adapting and evolving over time. Our shared co-emergence produces our interconnectedness, our interdependency, our Oneness.

D the Diversity: We are blessed with a novel-seeking universe. The great diversity we see on all physical scales—through our telescopes, our microscopes, and our own eyes—is a manifestation of just how creative our universe is! The great diversity we see around us stimulates our own imaginations and inspires our diversity of creative expression and thought. Diversity is precious. I like to think of the emergence of diversity as the ongoing story of creation. Our universe, including humankind and planet Earth, have not been created, but rather are creating. At any point in time, our "state of diversity" is the stage—the context—upon which further creating will occur.

I have a dream—really a prayer. My dream is that GOD—the Good, the Oneness, the Diversity—fully enters the consciousness of all of us as we live out our daily lives and make our daily choices. My dream is that GOD becomes our shared vision, highly valued—indeed, loved—by us all. My dream is that GOD becomes our shared framework for finding the solutions so desperately needed by humankind and Earth at this time. My dream is that such a shared vision, a shared framework, is the true gift which we give forward to what comes after us.

Dennis Hunter
Retired businessman

Betty Peck, in this wonderful work, *A Kindergarten Teacher Looks at the Word God*, invites us to reflect on one of the most important challenges, if not the most important challenge facing the world—facing America in particular. That challenge is to create oneness in the face of ever-increasing diversity.

Few times in history has one nation been in such a dominant economic and military position and simultaneously believed itself to be so threatened. No large-scale society has achieved such material abundance but been so poor in spirit. Perhaps not since ancient Athens or the Roman Republic has a society been bequeathed such a richness of foundational principles and yet been so bitterly divided and so fearful. If we are to heal this country and be to the world what John Winthrop and Ronald Reagan claimed us to be, the shining city on the hill, then we will need to find a renewed sense of common purpose and shared destiny. This will be no small task for a country riven by such dissension, but it would be impossible to forge a lasting vision without the participation and contribution of all diverse elements. And the current mean-spirited polarizing nature of our dialogue should give us an awareness of how far we have to go.

Betty's call, a call I have been privileged to hear for twenty years, to see the possibility for humankind in the working of nature, provides a possible and needed way out of the wilderness. Seen from the perspective of the ecology, of the whole, we come to understand that the greater the individual genetic diversity, the greater the resilience of the ecology, the whole.

Throughout time, the earth's environment has been in a state of flux, mostly gradual but occasionally cataclysmic, such as when it has been struck by a meteor. The greater the number of species, the higher the probability that life would survive in the new circumstances. So too it is with us.

Never has the pace of change been as rapid. Never, perhaps, have we felt so helpless and less in charge of our own destiny. In response, we seek someone to lead us through the travails. We seek certainty and come to see all those of different belief systems, whether they be religious, economic, or political, as potential adversaries. We seek to limit diversity, to demonize others. But these "others" have all arrived at this point in time with different experiences, different traditions and beliefs. Each of these ways of thinking has survived, in most cases for millennia. Each has something authentic to teach us. Each has the capacity of broadening our view of what is possible. And if we can expand the range of possibilities, we can increase our chances for survival if not success.

The older I have grown, the more I have come to believe two things. First, little in life can be accomplished alone. Any task of significance requires the cooperation of others. It is therefore in my self-interest to enlist the help of others in important tasks. And the prerequisite, other than obtaining compliance through force, is to achieve commitment by first treating "the other" with trust and respect. The second belief I have come to hold is that each of us, to a much greater degree than almost any of us is willing to accept, is the creator of our own reality rather than the victim of it. Space does not permit the development of this argument. All we need to consider is: if this statement is true, what does it mean about the responsibility each of us has to make the world a better place? As Gandhi said: *Be the change you wish to see in the world.* This advice makes little sense if we don't in fact create our own reality. Think about it.

I have been a businessman all my adult life. And I accept that that experience has created many prejudices within me that I struggle continuously to challenge. But it has also taught me some truths. One of those truths is that the possibilities available for consideration (the solution space) is frequently circumscribed by the way in which the problem/question is posed. For decades, the auto industry believed that high quality and low cost were opposed objectives. So the question always was: at what level would the design of a particular automobile under development trade off quality vs. cost? The tradeoff was different for a Cadillac than it was for a Chevrolet, but the tradeoff and the mindset that the tradeoff was inescapable were frozen in the way the question was asked. It took the Japanese to show us that the way to the lowest cost was in fact to drive for the highest quality. They showed us that the "genius of the AND" would beat "the tyranny of the OR."

It is armed with this understanding that we must face the challenge Betty Peck here puts before us. John Gardner, Secretary of Health, Education and Welfare during the Johnson administration, addressed this challenge in his commencement address to the 1991 graduating class at Stanford University:

> In the contemporary world, a community of any size has within it diverse sub-communities, so the problem is to achieve wholeness incorporating diversity.
>
> The goal is not to achieve wholeness by suppressing diversity, nor to make wholeness impossible by enthroning diversity, but to preserve both. Each element in the diversity must be respected, but each must ask itself sincerely what it can contribute to the whole. I don't think it is venturing beyond the truth to say that "wholeness incorporating diversity" defines the transcendent task of our generation.

Betty calls us to an awakening, calls us to come to our senses If we heed the call we are likely to be no less disoriented than was Rip Van Winkle after his twenty-year sleep. But if we are to leave a legacy deserving of our forebears' faith in us, then awake we must.

Richard House
Senior Lecturer in Psychotherapy and Counseling
Roehampton University, London, UK

May the Power of Love Triumph over the Love of Power

The Good, Oneness, and Diversity—how our post-modern culture is desperately crying out for an intelligent and sensitive embracing of these qualities today. In a world that is ravaged by myopic prejudice and ideological fundamentalism, by crassly one-sided materialism and unspeakably powerful commercial interests, it is becoming very difficult to keep faith in the simple virtues of love, honesty, and truth. It's not that these virtues have been completely lost to and through "modernity," but (as George Steiner so poignantly described), rather like the Nazis who engaged with the highest artistic sensibilities amidst their routine daily atrocities, it seems that (to take just a few examples) the modern-day executive and the party politician have similarly "split off" these virtues from their daily working lives, such that a loveless utilitarianism and a mechanistic "managerialism" dominate, with the values of love and honesty that our world so desperately needs being virtually absent from their day-to-day working existence. What I want to say here is centrally about children; I believe that a change in our relationship with children (especially around learning and schooling) is one of the central and most urgent spiritual imperatives of our times.

I am very fortunate to work with young children in Rudolf Steiner educational settings—and I am struck by how trustingly and unself-consciously young children model these qualities of being. There could hardly be a better example of how much we adults—trapped within our hyperactive lifestyles and materialistic preoccupations—have to learn from our children. What an ego-centred arrogance to assume that it is we adults who possess the requisite knowledge and wisdom for living, and that it is appropriate that our hapless children should be the recipients of it. Over the ages, the great spiritual masters have recognized that it is children who hold the deepest wisdom of all about living and loving; and there is an urgent need for educational systems across the globe to rediscover this perennial wisdom, and to find ways of seamlessly weaving it into our parenting and educational schooling practices. For as long as our schooling systems privilege utilitarian, instrumental learning ("high stakes" testing, education for "the needs of the economy") at the expense of the human soul and spirit, modern culture will continue to degenerate into a parlous vortex of our own making.

There is a paradox (and no doubt more than one!) at the heart of the modern age. In reality, and as we become ever more rooted in the materialistic, technological age, for much of the time we adults simply don't know. Indeed, if we are honest with ourselves and can momentarily rise above our anxieties, and as we increasingly lose touch with the spiritual world in the face of materialism's unforgiving ascendancy, uncertainty is surely the norm. Yet we are driven by our existential anxieties (often unwittingly) to self-deludingly insist upon knowing, manipulative control, predictability—and power. Power, too, is saturated in paradox. Not least, it is only when we can undefensively admit to our powerlessness at the deepest level that we will then re-member it in a new and far more wholesome, non-abusive way.

Returning to children, in my own experience it is those teachers who have the natural, unaffected humility to know that they don't know, and to find a way of relating with children which can "hold" this uncertainty, without generating anxiety in the process, or fleeing into a false, chimerical certainty, who are the most effective teachers—and the most successful "midwives" of the kind of wise and mature adulthood that this world so desperately needs.

It's not as if these understandings aren't already out there in the world: James Hillman, Robert Sardello, Donald Winnicott, Carl Rogers, David Michael Levin, Rudolf Steiner.... There is an almost endless lexicon of authorities whose precious work has given us the requisite insights. But do we as yet have the necessary individual and collective capacity to "own" our woeful shortcomings and (as Samuel Beckett had it) to "fall better"?... It is arguably in the spheres of parenting and educating our children that the most urgent transformation in consciousness is required. And if existential despair is, in some sense, the mother of spiritual invention, then perhaps the anomie and nihilism of our hyper-modern age are a necessary harbinger of and prerequisite for the kind of evolutionary leap in human consciousness that is perhaps the yearning wish of all contributors to this precious book.

Brenda Laurel
Author, Chair of the Graduate Program in Design
California College of Arts

Even as one who is not a theist, I am drawn to the exquisite visual and verbal interpretation of the sacred in this little book. Its spirit gives us an antidote to the destructive, polarizing energy that condenses around the word "GOD" in today's popular discourse. The three predominant patriarchal, monotheistic religions in the world today share the characteristic of privileging particular religious narratives as "truth" and denigrating others as "just stories." My spiritual practice has no gospel; it strives to see the truth within narratives that we call myths, folk tales, poetry—just stories. The ethos of the Druid bard—keeper of law and memory, harpist and teller of tales—encapsulates this value. My practice also honors science, characterized by Francis Bacon in his *Novum Organum* in 1620 as a "dialogue with nature." Through our conversations with the natural world, we both discover truths and unmask falsehoods, forming new narratives about life and the universe. Far from being the antithesis of science, narrative intelligence enables us to frame discourse and construct shared understanding, knowing that both the truths and the questions will change as our understanding grows. To some religious fundamentalists, the narratives of science are "just stories" as well. But over and over again in the history of humanity, narrative intelligence flows like water around the rocks of fundamentalism and dogma, generating new questions, new answers, and new ways of seeing.

In his book *Wonderful Life: The Burgess Shale and the Nature of History* [1989], Stephen Jay Gould posits that the two key traits that distinguish human beings from their forebears are abstract reasoning and representational art. Tool use was not sufficient for evolutionary success; other tool-using humanoid species have become extinct. Most of evolution's experiments end in failure. We are much more likely to die out than to transform into a self-aware, infinitely smart, infinitely wise collective being shrouded in white light. Extrapolating from Gould's observation, it may well be that the same set of traits that got us into the mess we've made of our planet are going to have to be the ones that get us out of it—namely, abstract reasoning and representational art. Through art and language, this book deconstructs G-O-D as a monolithic noun (that is, a word that must not be questioned) and redeploys the three letters as frames for ethical and spiritual ideas, with values, feelings, and beauty laced among them. In this book, the word is not enfolded in the cloak of religion, but rather opens out into a garden of ideas and images that nourish a mindful, soulful practice of living.

Gundi Heinemann
Educator, healing arts practitioner

Klaus Heinemann
Co-author of *The Orb Project*

Goodness Oneness Diversity

There is no need to delve into ancient scriptures to uncover this spiritual code. It's embedded in our genes (Gregg Braden. *The God Code*), and it's the message of unassuming visitors from the spiritual realm that more and more frequently show up in our digital photographs. It's the new paradigm.

Once G-O-D is embedded in our educational system so deeply that our children won't have forgotten it all by the time they enter college, the world will be a better place. Thank you, Betty Peck, for contributing to this critical paradigm shift.

Klaus

The word "God" stimulates a wide range of reactions in people of today. To some it pushes all their buttons, and they run away, without further interest in exploring the deeper meaning of this symbol of transformation. It takes the creativity of a director of Kindergarten education to help us remember the significance of the word. Young children are still in tune with "life is good." They spontaneously experience the innate goodness in numerous ways. They intuitively know that oneness is our highest purpose as they receive and express responsiveness/love or "quick give" daily. Most children still have a natural sense of awe and wonder and marvel at and explore with great curiosity the magnificent diversity all around us. They follow the plan that life's intentions are good, that we are one human family living on one planet Earth, our home; and that diversity is part of the grand design to keep us strong and able to work together for the benefit of all. With this message brought to light, G-O-D is our code for well-being.

Thank you, Betty, for presenting, uniquely packaged, the key to our future in its simplicity.

Gundi

Robert B. Louden
Professor of Philosophy
University of Southern Maine

Aristotle, in his *Metaphysics*, says that philosophy begins in wonder:

> For it is owing to their wonder that human beings both now begin and at first began to philosophize; they wondered originally at the obvious difficulties, then advanced little by little and stated difficulties about the greater matters, e. g., about the phenomena of the moon and those of the sun and the stars, and about the genesis of the universe (I.2 982b 11-17).

However, compulsory schooling, which existed nowhere in Aristotle's day (384-322 BCE) but which at present is nearly universal, is not generally known for its ability to cultivate wonder. We live in a schooled world now, but human beings' innate capacities to wonder, examine, and reflect are often being extinguished by the very institutions that are expected to educate them.

It is not that schools need to produce more professional philosophers, or that schools themselves are a bad idea, but simply that things don't always turn out as we had hoped. Modernity's commendable goal of eradicating illiteracy has also unintentionally contributed to a pervasive estrangement from the joy of learning. The battle against illiteracy has been won, but the price has been extremely high. Too many students graduate from educational institutions with their sense of wonder extinguished. And if Socrates is right when he says that "the unexamined life is not worth living" (*Apology* 38a), the quality of life that they have to look forward to after graduation will be bleak.

Kindergarten teachers stand in the front ranks of education, and because their students are not (yet) alienated from learning, they would seem to have a better chance of successfully cultivating a sense of wonder in their students. (By the time students work with a college or university professor, they are often deaf to the joy of learning, and have come to value education merely as a *Brotstudium*—a way to earn their bread and butter, not to mention the more expensive accoutrements of our consumer society).

But it takes a rare combination of talent, skill, desire, and patience to achieve this crucial goal, and not all teachers have it. Betty Peck has spent a lifetime cultivating wonder in her students (not all of whom were in her Kindergarten classes)—wonder not only about God, the Good, and the oneness as well as diversity of life, but also about gardens, food, art, music, drama, poetry, and a host of other matters that enrich daily life. She looks at things differently, but in my experience—as well as in that of those who have had the good fortune to know her—it is a kind of looking that makes all the difference.

Therese May
Quilt artist, educator

Good—What is good? God is Good

Compassion is good, and loving myself is good. I love myself! I love my creativity, and that is good. I love the idea that I always have choice and that I can choose the thoughts that I think. I can choose compassion, and that is good. I can choose forgiveness, and that is good. I can choose affirmative prayer, and that is good. What I find really good is that I can decide to find the good in all the situations in life. I can remember to breathe; I can meditate and communicate; I can listen to music, light a candle, and I can make a pot of soup. I can choose love and peace; I can surrender to love and peace; I can make a cup of tea and contemplate and extend my heart and hands to create world peace, and that is good!

Oneness—What is oneness? God is Oneness.

Oneness, the unity of all life, is peace, the end of suffering. It is understanding and communication, the connection of all souls in integrity and wholeness. It is infinite balance, equality—the universal peace, world peace, life itself. There is no separation, no war, no resistance, no beginning, and no end—forever and ever in eternity, eternal light, eternal life. Forgiving. Hearts and hands creating, building bridges.

Diversity—What is diversity? God is Diversity.

I see a beautiful pattern with contrast: light and shadow, a complete variety of colors of the spectrum from one end to the other. There are shapes and sizes of shapes and different shapes and colors of shapes with shading. There are points of view—good and bad and in-between—puzzle parts making up a complete picture, patches of a quilt, parts of a body, musical notes up and down, songs with many feelings—happy, sad, mad, bland—cultures, languages, animals, plants, people, insects, minerals, earth, air, fire, water, mountains, valleys, intelligence, personality characteristics—all taking shape—four seasons blending into one—inner and outer space.

Dorothy Hewes
Professor in the Department of Child and Family Development
San Diego State University

Our Father's God

Friedrich Froebel is often referred to as the Father of the Kindergarten, but success did not come until near the end of his difficult life. He was born April 21, 1782, in the Prussian village of Oberweissbach. His mother died soon afterward, and his overworked father was a minister to several Lutheran churches. Because of a reading problem, young Friedrich was enrolled in the local school for girls, where lessons consisted mainly of memorizing Bible passages. (To the end of his life, he could remember the one they shouted together on his first day, "Seek ye first the kingdom of God and his righteousness, and all these things shall be added unto you.") At age ten he was taken into the home of an uncle, and for the next five years he went to a boys' school where he felt that the memorized assignments taught virtually nothing. Apprenticing with a forester and work on the country estates introduced him to the natural world. In an 1837 autobiographical letter, he wrote that his "religious life now changed to a religious communion with nature" and that "the oneness of all nature" dawned upon him.

In 1805, Froebel's uncle died and left him enough money to study at several universities. One was in Jena, where he was introduced to newly translated books of Asian religions. They were in such sharp contrast with the Lutheran Bible that his approach to teaching was forever influenced. Also, his studies in crystallography at the University of Berlin revealed that their interior structure determined the unique final shape of each crystal. He later used this in developing a theory that children's learning also must take place within them, instead of being imposed by the teacher or other outside influence. For several years he drifted from one place and one job to another. Then, in 1804, an acquaintance persuaded him to become a teacher. His first classes were with young boys, and he later wrote that he felt as if he had found something he had always longed for: "I felt as happy as the fish in the water, the bird in the air."

At this time, few parents considered children's developmental needs. They were seen as "blank slates" upon which adults were to impress those things necessary for life on earth and in heaven. Corporal punishment was believed necessary to achieve conformity, both at school and at home, following the biblical injunction that to spare the rod was to spoil the child. By the end of the 1700s, a time of philosophical and governmental changes, a few educators began to question this need for severe punishment. One of these was Pestalozzi. After spending two years at his school in Yverdon, Switzerland, Froebel opened The Universal German Educational Institution in rural Greisheim in 1816. He enrolled both boys and girls, at a time when coeducation was a radical idea. Instead of corporal punishment, students who misbehaved found a single slice of bread on their dinner plate. During this period, with the assistance of his wife, Froebel wrote *The Education of Man* to explain his system. (The German word that was translated as "Man" actually meant both sexes.) It has subsequently become the best known source of his ideas.

The young students were happy at his boarding school, and many of them remained supporters when they became adults, but Froebel came to recognize that they were under-prepared for their studies when they cam to him at age seven. He began correspondence and research to determine what might be done to remedy this. In this process, he discovered the forgotten writings of Comenius. Although that method of birth-to-formal-education was for mothers to use at home, it gave Froebel the incentive to develop a school for young children. His first attempts were in Blankenberg in the 1830s.There were already "infant schools" as day-care centers for poor working mothers, but he didn't want to be identified with them. After much pondering over the name, it came to him as he walked with friends across a mountain road. He had been comparing children to young plants in a garden, needing nourishment to grow to their potential, and *Kindergarten* was the term he chose. He officially opened the first one in 1840 and began traveling to other cities to encourage others.

Although there were always financial difficulties, Kindergartens spread throughout Europe. Froebel's philosophy became recognized by the education leaders and other influential European leaders. In 1848, he began training young women as teachers, at a time when this was unheard of. This not only set a precedent that led to the acceptance of females entering the previously male world of teaching older children but was an important first step to higher education. Although other locations were not affected, the Kindergarten dream came to an abrupt halt when the Prussian Minister of Education published an edict on August 7, 1851, which ordered all Kindergartens under his jurisdiction to be closed because they were part of a system "calculated to train the youth of the country to atheism" and could not be allowed to exist. (While it was not mentioned, the education of women as teachers was apparently one of the factors involved.) Despite efforts by other government officials and Kindergarten advocates, this ban remained in effect for six years. Although he was deeply discouraged, Froebel continued his efforts. In 1852, he attended the European educators' conference, where his entrance was greeted by a standing ovation, and he enjoyed a seventieth birthday party in April. Then he became bedridden, and it was said that his death on June 21 was caused by a broken heart.

This edict, coming at a time of political upheaval in what was then the independent kingdom of Prussia, actually served to strengthen the Kindergarten. Within Europe, supporters rallied around the movement and others joined them. Political liberals had begun to emigrate after an aborted revolution in 1848, and even Froebel talked of going to the United States. Several of his former students who came to the United States in the 1850s opened Kindergartens for German-speaking children, but by the 1870s there were both preschool programs and teacher training schools. Some went to England, where they participated in the 1854 International Exhibition of Educational Systems. After attending it, Henry Barnard, Connecticut publisher of educational materials, wrote an enthusiastic report that introduced the concept to American educators. The number of Froebelian-based Kindergartens for children aged three to seven continued to grow with private sponsorship until the twentieth century. At that time the public schools began to incorporate them, but only for the year before the first grade. In the 1920s, Patty Smith Hill, a Froebelian faculty member at Teacher's College, Columbia University, organized a Committee on Nursery Schools to provide for younger children. It has evolved into the National Association for the Education of Young Children (NAEYC) which has maintained Froebel's basic principles.

Froebel had developed an educational system based upon his observations of developmental levels. Nature is a manifestation of God, he said as early as the 1820s, but it must be seen as a continuously interconnected whole that requires the guidance of adults. To develop children's minds, Froebel devised a series of what became known as the Gifts and Occupations. Eventually the concept of "workful play and playful work" was restored in American Kindergartens. The small wooden blocks that were originally used individually on tables became unit blocks for group constructions on the floor. Observations of the hanging cube and sphere were replaced by the stringing of wooden beads. Art was considered valuable, with slates replaced by crayons and later by easel and paints. Songs and activities were often revised to make them more relevant to modern children, and new ones were written. (For example, "Happy Birthday to You" was composed in 1886 by Patty Smith Hill and is sung around the world to this day.)

But how did Froebel view God? This was a time of conflict between Catholics and Lutherans, and Froebel did not identify with either denomination. His basic concept was that every child is born with a love of God and that this needs to be supported and developed. One of the most detailed discussions of this topic is a chapter in Bowen's *Froebel and Education Through Self-Activity*, written in 1892. He begins by quoting a conversation between Froebel and a companion as they rode in an open carriage on a clear, starry night. Froebel said: "The firmament leads us to recognize the connectedness of all that exists, and leads us up to unity—which is God. Just as there is an interconnectedness among the stars, so is this the common life-principle here on earth." From boyhood he had delighted in the world of plants and flowers. When he became a student of physical science he was constantly awed by the regularity of nature. To him, nature became the Book of God designed for our learning. To properly read it, the senses must be awakened from birth onward. The aim of every educator should not be mere book-learning. It should be through actions such as gardening, because this gives children awareness of an unseen power, and a sense of responsibility that is the basis of moral culture. Physical and spiritual development should be united from earliest childhood, and it is best demonstrated through play that demonstrates some idea. Creativity is essential. Merely following the rules set by others does not lead to understanding. Was Froebel actually a pantheist? When asked that question, he replied that the pantheists say that the world is God's body, that God lives in it a in a house. Instead he believed that the spirit of God dwells in nature as the "common life principle" for every person to discover. He did not expect children to memorize Bible verses or sing hymns, but he strongly advocated learning experiences that led to this basis for lifelong unity with the universe.

Mary Ellen Mark
Registered Nurse, LaC, D.O.M.

I am rather anti-organized religion. After having been brought up in the Catholic Church and having spent my fourth grade year in a jail in Tarrytown, New York, I have questioned religion, going back to my first brush with the indoctrination by the nuns in preparation for my first communion at age 6. It seemed to be downhill from then until we went to East Africa, and I met some fascinating people who looked at God as being everything and everywhere. In Ethiopia the churches were mainly for meditation, with the ceiling being covered with round doll-like faces, encircled with masses of curly black hair, each with wings sprouting from the non-existent shoulder area.

The overwhelming peace I still carry with me over forty years later is coupled with my next encounter in Kenya and Tanzania with the awesome starkness and beauty of the game parks. This is a belief system that tells of God in every living creature, blade of grass, color of the land, breathtaking sunrises and sunsets. There I looked at the landscape of God. The feelings and majesty cannot be captured on any edifice, no matter how grand or overflowing with people.

God is a place within our eyes, our breath, and all of the movements we make. It is an overwhelming feeling that we must nurture from our first intake of air to our last exhale. It is uncomplicated, non-judging, and full of hope for ourselves and everything on this planet. It is joyful, has a love that is boundless, that encompasses everything we know and all that we do not know. God is peace. When we touch each other, we feel the power of every breath, every joy and sorrow. We need each other and the power of the universe to surround us with peace, which brings the Goodness into the Oneness of all life and enhances the Diversity.

Nancy Payne
Registered Nurse, writer

On putting the other "o" back into the word God

Good. People seem to have forced the issue, insisting that God be a good god. Thus, the two words seem to be the same. I feel it is a very Good Idea to put that second (or first) "o" back into the word God—and if it really wasn't there at first, it is time it becomes so.

Oneness—the Great Oneness. Here we are at the first and second "o" again. At this stage of our Global Game, Oneness is having to be pointed out and taught to everyone. How sad! Kids in school—high school, middle school, college—to police, politicians, preachers, and persons of every ilk. There is but ONE race. Please get your papers and card now. Our DNA shows but very few and slight differences—and it does not reveal what color, creed, or culture you happen to embrace physically. We are all made of the SAME stardust, planetdust, galaxydust, Uni/Versedust. And so is the Flora. And this just barely covers the physical realm. A very few semi-understand the spiritual Oneness that exists in all things. Many are beginning to seek this understanding now, but even then it is followed through in the physical realm they inhabit. In our beginnings, we all look alike. We need to expand this from our global garden out into the feeling visions of all planes of the Uni/Verse…until we reach the Great Oneness, the Center of centers, Source of sources, The Great Poobah, or the Great Whatever…all One and the Same.

The infinite mind really does not comprehend a story without a beginning, a middle without an end, so going back to that beginning (which may not even be there) may be futile, but we can search for the One-ness. So it is that **no** finite mind can really know the great mysterium of the Uni/Verse in truth—the double "o", Double Oneness of g-o-o-d. We might have to place one "o" on top of the other to achieve a magnification of the g-o-o-d in our "little o" word.

Diversity is the stuff of survival, enduringness, infinity. Without it, just where would collectors be? What would they do? The world would certainly be boring and fragile. It is Annie Dillard talking about the "profligate extravagance of nature—the Uni/Verse." "It will try anything once." She describes God as a "megalomaniac with unlimited capital." What she is describing is the incredible abundance and possibility (diversity) that is Uni/Verse. All of us in human form—of many colors and hues, many minds and cultures, many belief systems and attitudes, many songs—are all here, and the combinations that are possible are endless.

Diversity is the O-neness, is the G-ood.

Emory J. Michael
Author of *Queen of the Sun* and *The Alchemy of Sacred Living*

The great mystery that has challenged humanity since the dawn of time—the secrets of life, existence and creation—all these and more are contained in the simple word *God.* Perhaps no other word so lends itself to a consideration of its meaning when looked on as an acronym.

God is Good. In his search for truth, the ancient Greek philosopher Plato gave us the philosophical ideals of goodness, truth and beauty. Goodness has from the dawn of time been considered an essential attribute of God, and it is likely no accident that the English word for God so closely resembles the word *good*, for "God is good."

Children learn about God from their parents and teachers. Children want to know that the world is good, that the universe has a heart, and that there is safety in the care and watchfulness of loving adults. Adults communicate to a child in countless subtle ways a message as to the nature of the world. It is the task of all those who teach young children to convey to them through word and deed, story and song, the realization in their young, impressionable hearts that the world they live in is good. Later, we learn that life is governed by a subtle natural or spiritual law, and that the law of causation holds sway in human affairs. What we do to our neighbor is the most important event of any moment. And as a result of the reciprocity at the heart of all action, what we do to another we do to ourselves. When we live from the heart, our lives are blessed and in turn bless others. When our hearts are full of love, we are friends with the universe, and live in a world that is good.

God is Oneness. In many ancient cultures people believed that "man is a microcosm," that is, the human world is a reflection of the world of the gods, or God. They believed that we ourselves have our existence in the totality of divine life—it is in God that we live, move and have our being. In other words, we all have our origins in the universal life force, that indescribable essence and creative intelligence that brought the universe into being.

The Celtic knot is a most eloquent symbol of the interconnectedness and intertwining relationship of all living things. Celtic knots interweave in an intricate pattern without beginning or end. This suggests that the life force with which we are endowed—as well as the unfolding pattern of our lives and relationships—is inscrutable in origin and endless in its outreach. Not only do we live and move and have our being in the great mystery, but all of us are linked together in a chain of interconnected relationship, without beginning or end.

This suggests that we influence each other by all that we say and do, for the fabric of life is an unbroken field, a finely interwoven tapestry of interconnectedness. Rather than to say "we are all one," perhaps it would be more accurate to say that "we are all part of the one." Our lives are an intricate part of a greater whole. And if what the quantum physicists tell us is true, our thoughts, words, and deeds carry an influence that reaches to the farthest star. We are all making ripples in the same pond.

God is Diversity. Nature displays an endless liberality in its cornucopia of forms—an inexhaustible overflowing exuberance in the creative ideas tried out by the evolving life force. The creative genius that brought the world into being obviously delights in variety—a kaleidoscope of infinite diversity. No two creatures are exactly alike. No two butterflies exactly repeat nature's pattern; no feather, face or fingerprint is identical to another.

So too, each human being is profoundly unique. We are all playing in the same game, but we don't all play the same position. Yet each one's contribution is essential. Just as we are all held together in nature's resplendent interweaving, so do we each carry a gift of our own uniqueness. Everyone matters. No thing, no event, is too small to be of consequence. Thankfully, we have only to concern ourselves with our own little corner. If we make our own garden bloom, we may rest assured that we will have made the world a better place.

April Halberstadt
Mother, writer, historian

Words are such a poor medium
to describe
the marvelous Power that surges within us,
that flows among us,
that makes me One with all life.

From the plankton in the ocean,
to the mind of a genius,
the Power of God is within us all.

The Power comes from a past
too distant for me to fathom,
and the Power goes beyond
to an eternity without measure.

How can we know and understand such a Power?
How do we encounter God?
Although I see His hand in the natural wonders of this world,
I feel His presence most often
in the creative act.

When I hear wonderful music,
feel a loving act,
see an artistic masterpiece,
eat a fabulous meal, or
enjoy a beautiful book,
I am witness to the Power of the soul of another.

As I go about my day, I welcome
opportunities to encounter this Power,
finding it often while gardening—and
I see it frequently in the creativity of others.

I join with others in practicing the Roman Catholic
rituals of my family, parents and grandparents,
and I believe in the community of all
who search for the Power.

And so it is with great pleasure that I participate
in the Creativity and the Goodness
of this project, finding a wondrous expression
of Perfect Love in the art, the words, and
the creative spirits that make it possible.

Thoughts for further Contemplation

We are indebted to Harold Mellor Hodges, former head of the Department of Sociology and Anthropology at San Jose State University and guest professor at other universities, for his contribution of thought-provoking statements by people from many cultures at various periods of history. This gives us another evocative picture of unity within the diversity of the human spirit. We have drawn on the much more extensive contemplation that Mr. Hodges has made on the many ramifications of the idea of the sacred or spiritual. Here we present quotations most closely related to the themes of this small book.

Reverence for life . . . is the source of constant renewal
for the individual and for humankind.

—Albert Schweitzer

Just to be is a blessing.
Just to live is holy.

—Rabbi Abraham Heschel

God

I could not say I believe. I *know!*
I have had the experience of being
Gripped by something that is
Stronger than myself, something
That people call God.

—Albert Einstein

Divine Love always has met and
Always will meet every human need.

—Mary Baker Eddy

God is an angel in an angel
And a stone in a stone
And a straw in a straw.

—John Donne

Nothing exists, save God.

—Sufi saying

Goodness

Goodness needeth not to enter into the soul,
For it is already there, only to be perceived.

—*Theologia Germanica*

Prove all things; hold fast that which is good.

—St. Paul
I Thessalonians 5:21

Be not overcome of evil,
but overcome evil with good.

—St. Paul
Romans 12:21

Virtue is bold, and goodness never fearful.

—Shakespeare
Measure for Measure III, I, 214

Ring out false pride in place and blood,
  The civic slander and the spite;
  Ring in the love of truth and right,
Ring in the common love of good.

—Alfred Lord Tennyson

In the world of knowledge, the essential Form of Good is the limit of our inquiries, and can barely be perceived; but, when perceived, we cannot help concluding that it is in every case the source of all that is bright and beautiful.

—Plato
The Republic, Book 7, 517

The greatest thing to learn is the idea of good.

—Plato
The Republic, 505a

Good is it to repeat and review what is good.

—Plato
Gorgias, 498e

Oneness

A single spirit fills infinity.
It is that of God, whom nothing
Limits or divides, who is everywhere,
Entire and never confined.

—Eliphas Levi

God is a circle whose center is every-
where and its circumference nowhere.

—Empedocles

Outside of God there
is nothing but nothing.

—Meister Eckhart

Ultimately all the moments are really one.
Therefore now is eternity . . . everything,
including me, is dying every moment
into eternity and being born again.

—David Bohm, physicist

I am one with the rain pattering
on the roof of the cloud floating
in the sky. No longer "I" and "It"
or "I" and "thou," but only "is."

—William Johnston

We do not have solitary beings. Every creature is, in some sense, connected to, dependent on the rest.

—Lewis Thomas

Diversity

If we are to live together in peace, we must come to know each other better.

—Lyndon Baines Johnson

Uniformity is not nature's way; diversity is nature's way.

—Vandana Shiva

We are all full of weaknesses and errors; let us mutually pardon each other our follies—it is the law of nature.

—Voltaire

My humanity is bound up in yours, for we can only be human together

—Archbishop Desmond Tutu

Peace is not unity in similarity but unity in diversity, in the comparison and conciliation of differences.

—Mikhail Gorbachev

Freedom rings whenever opinions clash.

—Adlai Stevenson

When we lose the right to be different, we lose the privilege to be free.

—Charles Evans Hughes
Chief Justice of the U.S. Supreme Court

...and diversity leads to the oneness

There can be hope only for a society which acts as one big family, not as many separate ones.

—Anwar Sadat

The wise man belongs to all countries, for the home of a great soul is the whole world.

—Democritus

No one is born hating another person because of the color of his skin, or his background, or his religion. If [people] can learn to hate, they can be taught to love, for love comes more naturally to the human heart than its opposite.

—Nelson Mandela

Everyone in the world smiles in the same language

—Mexican-American proverb

E pluribus unum

—Motto of the United States of America

Nature

But ask now the beasts, and they shall teach thee;
And the birds of the air, and they shall tell thee:

—Job 12:7

Mist rising from the water is prayer.
Nature has allegories of her own.

—Novalis

The earth, our mother, is telling us to behave.

—the Dalai Lama

When we abuse nature, we abuse ourselves.

—Chatsumaru Kabilsingh

Holy Earth Mother, the trees
and all nature are witnesses
of your thoughts and deeds.

—Winnebago prayer

My father considered
a walk among the trees
the equivalent
of churchgoing.

—Aldous Huxley

Nature is part of us, we are part of it.
We can recognize ourselves
In the descriptions we give of it.

—Ilya Prigogine,
Nobel Laureate (Chemistry)

The air, blowing everywhere, serves all creatures.

—Hildegard of Bingen

Children

Unless you change and become as little children,
you will never enter into the kingdom of heaven.

—Jesus
Matthew 18:3

Let parents then bequeath to their children
not riches, but the spirit of reverence.

—Plato
Protagoras, 729A